"When you reach up for the Lord's power in your life with the same intensity that a drowning person has when grasping and gasping for air, power from Jesus Christ will be yours."

–President Russell M. Nelson, "Drawing the Power of Jesus Christ into Our Lives," April 2017 General Conference

Come
Unto Me

"It is mentally rigorous to strive to look unto Him in every thought. But when we do, our doubts and fears flee."

–President Russell M. Nelson, "Let God Prevail," October 2020 General Conference

Made in United States
Troutdale, OR
12/17/2024

26774132R00063